# CHOSEN
# FOR
# BATTLE

**Debbie Watson-Allen**

DAYELight
**PUBLISHERS**

ISBN: 978-1-949343-61-8

# Acknowledgment

This book was birth from the experiences God allowed me to go through, including my journey with breast cancer. I want to honor God, who chose me to go through these experiences and granted me the grace and mercy of deliverance.

Special thanks to my friends and family, who prayed with me through my times of trials, and they were relentless in their faith for me.

Sincere gratitude to Winsome Brown, my mother, who prayed for me through my challenging days. She was an inspiration to me in writing this book, and she was always persistent in asking how the book was coming along.

To the one who inspired me, my daughter-in-law, Donica Blackwood-Allen, who believed in me to write this book. She encouraged me to write the book, even before I had the thought. When I decided to write it, she helped me to find a book coach.

Thanks to my church family, who prayed with and encouraged me through my time of illness.

# Table of Contents

# Chosen

You are chosen because there is a purpose within you.

You are chosen because God wants to elevate you to the next level in your faith.

You are chosen because the devil sees you and wants to stop you.

You are chosen to lift up others.

You are chosen because God wants to shift you in the spiritual realm.

You are chosen because your destiny will bring others to their destiny.

You are chosen because of the coverage that has been placed upon you.

You are chosen because you can enlighten others. God wants to move you, as you have never been moved before.

So, walk in your purpose. Step out of your comfort zone, and let your chosen purpose be seen and heard.

Let your chosen purpose propel someone else's purpose.

Let God be seen in you; let God shine through you.

Let God move through you.

Walk in your purpose.

~ Debbie Watson-Allen

Life, as it is, is full of circumstances that will put our faith to the test. One may question their faith amid their trials and wonder why these things are happening to them. I realized that, just like Job, I was chosen for the different battles in my life and I want to share some of them with you. I hope you realize that you too have been chosen. I know it is hard right now, so I hope this book will help you fight for the freedom you want and be the best God has called you to be.

# Introduction

The enemy doesn't play fair; there is no such thing as fair game to him. He seeks to destroy, and he will do everything within his powers to accomplish that which he seeks to do, so do not ever think that you are not a target. You are not a target, only if you are already his.

The battle for ultimate control of your every senses is his target. He is the destroyer of souls and his attacks are countless. His attacks are untimely, and he never takes a break. Like the game of dominoes, he plays as one who is a "cut-throat." He is ruthless in his attacks, and he will attack, even if you are wounded. There is no compassion in him for you; he is merciless. The enemy is relentless in his endeavor to conquer at any cost, pursuing with vengeance and bile. He seeks to weary you, so you lose all control and faith in yourself and faith in the almighty God.

How will this fight play out, when your back is against the wall, and there is the feeling that all odds are against you? Are you going to give up? Are you going to fight?

Are you going to lose faith in the one true Savior and ultimate Healer? The enemy will never give you time to think or recover, so you must be in sync with your Lord at all times. You should not be content with just a mere feeling but have that strong conviction and affirm that God is always with you. Therefore, having a constant relationship with Christ, your Savior, is important. Do not allow that constant communing with Him to go dim but be persistent at all times. Let the words of the Lord abide in your heart. It was David who said:

> *Thy word is a lamp unto my feet, and a light unto my path.* (Psalm 119:105).

It is the word of the Lord that will guide you. God is the Word, according to John 1:1:

> *In the beginning was the Word, and the Word was with God, and the Word was God.*

We cannot separate the Word from God; the two are the same. The Psalmist, David, says he hides the Word in his heart that he will not sin against God (Psalm 119:11). It is, therefore, fitting that when trials and temptation come your way, hold fast to the Word of God so you sin not.

When the children of Israel were going through the wilderness, they murmured about everything; nothing

12

was satisfying to them. They complained about being taken out of Egypt where they had flesh and bread (Exodus 16:2-3). When they were given manna from heaven and quail, they still murmured. God was grieved with that generation. Hence, we have an example of what not to do. If you are faced with making a choice in the face of tribulation, it is not time to murmur but choose to call on your Savior and Deliverer, Jesus Christ. Murmuring will only cover your spiritual eyes, and you will not be able to see what God is doing or what He is about to do.

According to the Bible, the enemy, known as the devil, Satan or Lucifer, was once a decorated angel in heaven. He was the master of music and he was beautiful, but he allowed his pride to surpass that of the natural and sought to exalt himself above the Lord God of all things. Satan was thrown out of heaven, with one-third of the angels who cohered with him in trying to overthrow God. Satan is no god, but a "wannabe."

The enemy covets your relationship with God because his relationship was severed due to his lack of humility. He knows what is in store for you, and he doesn't want you to obtain it. The benefits of a relationship with God are endless because Jesus said He is from everlasting to everlasting (Psalm 41:13). God promises us peace, but not as the world giveth. He promises us everlasting life with Him, so He has gone to prepare a place for us, that where He is, we will also be.

The enemy will flood you with emotions of guilt or shame. You may feel unworthy and separated from God in times of trouble. Be encouraged that Jesus Christ shed His blood on Calvary so we can have life and live in liberty. When Jesus became the ultimate sacrifice for our sin, he bridged the gap of sin that separated us from God. Therefore, when we fall at God's mercy seat in prayer, God does not see our sins but His blood that was shed on Calvary. If God sees only the blood of Jesus, then He sees mercy crying out for us. There is this assurance that we can stand, knowing there is hope in our Savior, Jesus Christ.

You may be at a place where you feel like everything is going wrong; sickness on one side, and death on the other. You may want to blame yourself, thinking you must be doing something wrong. You need to push pause for a moment, then rewind. If you have not repented, then you need to repent of your sins. Repentance is vital for the washing of your sins by the blood of Jesus. Sin cannot stand before God, but the blood that is crying out for us can. Have you taken on the name of Jesus Christ by baptism and being filled with His Holy Spirit? When we accept Jesus Christ as our Lord and Savior, we take His name. His name is important because it is the only name given under heaven whereby men can be saved. If you receive a check for one million dollars, but there is no name on it, you cannot cash that check because it needs a name.

Are you walking according to the commandments of the Lord? If your answer is no, be assured, all is not lost. Jesus Christ has come that we may have life and life more abundantly. He has given us the blueprint, which is the Bible, to guide us in our walk with Him. His Word tells us how we should go about our everyday life. There are ways illustrated on how to handle the various encounters in life.

The enemy may remind you of your past in order to keep you trapped in a sinful cycle. If you remain in that state of constant repentance, you cannot live in the presence of the Lord. God has already forgiven you, so be free to praise Him. When you dwell in the past, your prayers are limited to prayers of constant repentance for the same thing. You will not grow in intercession in the Spirit. The Bible says that God inhabits the praises of His people, and we overcome by our praises and testimony (Revelation 12:11). Often, God has already forgiven us, but we refuse to forgive ourselves. Yet, the Word of the Lord says, if our hearts condemn us, God is bigger than our hearts (1 John 3:20).

# Chapter 1
## Training Ground

The time came when I was chosen for something greater than me. To be chosen is to be selected among the finest. The Webster dictionary defines "divine favor" as being given a special privilege. A chosen person is often handpicked based on their character or ability to perform. Selecting someone for a particular task is done with the expectation of a particular end as it relates to the task at hand. If you want something accomplished, you would not pick on someone with little or no knowledge and experience of the process.

You may think that the experiences you have had no actual meaning behind them. In every step of our lives, our experiences will build us. These experiences help to form our personalities and reactions. It is our experiences that will take us to another level in our faith. It is what you know that you will depend on in times of crisis. Therefore, when you reflect on your past experiences, what did you use as your defense?

Have you ever stopped to think that there must be training before the ultimate fight?

Let us examine a soldier as he prepares for war. It takes a lot of preparation and various tests. The preparation is not what the solider in training wants, but it is what is necessary. The training takes different forms to build resilience. The soldier must pass a test after every training event. The soldier's training is to build strength, while gaining stamina. The training is often rigorous and requires much discipline and determination. The soldier is not only prepared physically but mentally. The Bible refers to us as soldiers of the Lord. Hence, as soldiers, we must go through our training to become the kind of soldiers God wants us to be.

The things we accomplish are first won in our minds. According to the Bible, we are to be transformed by the renewing of our minds (Romans 12:2). It is, therefore, fitting that our thoughts are different when we become new in Christ Jesus. We must begin to think the way Christ thinks. Having this mindset will cause a dramatic change in how we view ourselves and our situation. The change in the thought process now brings about a change in one's actions. The positive mindset brings an outward posture that is upright and confident. The positive mindset will also speak positively.

The mind is very powerful, and it is the driving force for our actions and reactions. Before we act, the thoughts concerning that action have already been processed in our minds. That is why the Bible says a double-minded man is unstable in all his ways (James 1:8). The planned activities of a man must be in sync with his mind for a specific direction, and not be wavering. In the natural, the soldiers in the army are prepared in survival skills. They are prepared for combat, so they learn to defend themselves. The soldiers in the height of war cannot be wavering in what to do but must be precise because their lives and the lives of their comrades depend on it. They must decide to shoot or not shoot because one moment of hesitation could cost them their lives or the lives of their fellow comrades.

The Bible says the weapons of our warfare are not carnal but mighty in the pulling down of the strongholds of the enemy (2 Corinthians 10:4). It also states that we should put on the whole armor of God (Ephesians 6:11). The Lord knows that there will be battles in our lives and He wants to prepare us in every way. He, therefore, has given us the blueprint for what is needed. The armor of God gives us full protection as children of God, and we should not go to war without it.

The armor of God is found in Ephesians 6. It consists of:

- **The Gospel of Peace:** This is your salvation. It is your acceptance of Jesus Christ as your Lord and savior.

- **The Shield of Faith:** A shield, as we know it, is used in war to block the attack of the enemy. It is used to quench the fiery darts of the wicked, so when the enemy throws doubts and fears at us, we stand in our faith that God can. We trust in God's word and it speaks to our deliverance.

- **The Helmet of Salvation**. It is in knowing that we have deliverance from sin because Jesus Christ paid the price on the cross. It is that freedom we have in knowing who we are in Christ Jesus. It is walking with God by trusting His Word for direction in our lives.

- **The Sword of the Spirit**. This is the pure Word of God. The Bible says the Word is God (John 1:1). It also says the words of the Lord are purified seven times (Psalms 12:6). It also says God cannot lie (Numbers 23:19). If you trust in God, then you trust His Word. The Word gives guidance for hope, love, peace, healing, saving, deliverance and so much more. The sword is one that cuts and heals. In the spiritual realm, the Word brings healing, when you are wounded by the enemy. Yet, it is your weapon for an attack on the enemy.

The challenges in your life call for action, so what will you do at such times? Do you remember your first encounter with God being your Protector and Guide? What were your thoughts, while going through your struggles? Surely, we do not want to surrender to the enemy, but it is a fight that ends with a winner and that winner must be you. As a child of God, you have the greatest Champion of all on your side. He is the King of kings and Lord of lords, Jesus Christ. The soldier is never alone but always has support. The same is true in our spiritual battles: the Lord is our defense. He never leaves us or forsakes us.

> *For the Lord your God is he that goeth with you, to fight for you against your enemies, to save you.* (Deuteronomy 20:4 2).

We often find ourselves in our testing, but don't want to go through it. We might even have to repeat the test before we pass. However, passing is a must. We must learn spiritual survival skills so we can endure hardness, as good soldiers of Christ, according to the Bible (2 Timothy 2:3).

## *Spiritual Survival*

For our spiritual survival, we need to do what Jesus Christ did:

### 1. **Learn the Word:**

> *Study to show thyself approved unto God, a workman that needed not to be ashamed, rightly dividing the word of truth. (*2 Timothy 2:15).

The Word should never be taken for granted by a child of God. It is the Word that will come to your aid when the enemy attempts to back you in a corner. Jesus put the Word into effect as His defense when the enemy came and tempt Him after He came out of the wilderness. He was able to say: "It is written…" It is the written Word that came alive and pushed the enemy away. It was the Word that paralyzed him.

### 2. **Fasting and Prayer:**

Jesus went into the wilderness in fasting and prayer. He denied the flesh, to strengthen the spirit. That is a great example for us, as this flesh is often weak in faith and gravitates towards the carnal things. Jesus also prayed earnestly before He was taken to be crucified. He knew what was coming. He knew the outcome of His destiny on earth and that was impressed deeply on Him. It was

His death, burial, and resurrection that would change the hope of mankind into hope for eternity with Him.

### 3. **Be Separated:**

Being separated does not mean being alienated. The example that Jesus set was one of being in this world, but not caught up in the reveling of this world. He spent His time teaching His disciples and the multitude. He healed and delivered many. Yet, He said His duty was to be about His Father's business (Luke 2:49). Even though He was teaching and performing miracles, His main purpose was to die for our sins.

What threatens your survival? Are you surrounding yourself with the right people? Who is mentoring you? In answering these questions, take into consideration that your choice of a mentor can have a drastic effect on your outcomes. The people you choose to take advice from can make you or break you.

King David had his training in the field with his sheep. He was their defense against a lion and a bear. His instinct to protect was high. He did not fear for his life but made the step forward and defended those helpless sheep. When he visited his brothers on the battlefield, Goliath was present. David stood fearless, in the name of his Lord. He knew the capability of the God he trusts because he had proven Him in the back of the desert. David, therefore, stood boldly when his training was

23

now being put to the test. He was ready to defend the name of his God; to defend God's reputation and that of His army. David knew who he was in the Lord. His faith was in the One who gave him the strength to defend his sheep. David had strength in his loins because he had the truth.

Your experiences may come in many forms and shapes. Therefore, your choice of weapon for your particular battle is very important. God knows you and He has chosen you for your particular circumstances. Therefore, accept that:

1. **You are a child of God.** The rights of a child are granted to you when you accepted Jesus as your Lord and Savior. He said we are no longer servants but sons (Galatians 4:7). As a child of God, He becomes our heavenly Father, and He gives us gifts far better than our earthly fathers.

2. **He has chosen you for this battle.** He knows you can overcome because we are more than conquers in Christ Jesus (Romans 8:37). Numbers 6:24 says: "The Lord bless thee, and keep thee." If He blesses and keeps you, surely He will not let you die in the hands of the enemy. He will rescue you.

As a soldier, you can fight on the defensive as well as on the offense. I, personally, like to fight offense. I always want to be in control. I am not doing it on my own but doing it knowing that God is my defense. When you know who you are in Christ Jesus, you will live as such, and not let the enemy walk all over you. God said you are healed by His stripes (Isaiah 53:5) so why do you allow the enemy to tell you otherwise. He said you are the head and not the tail, according to Deuteronomy 28:44, so why should you be anything less than that. You must trust the Word of the One who is the head of your life. I do not want to take any chances with the enemy, so I do not entertain his lies. I am who God says I am and nothing less. We must wound the enemy before he wounds us. We do so with our praise to the Most-High, prayers, worship, and dedication to the Word of God. We must have a relationship with God. You must be ruthless in your offense position, leaving the enemy paralyzed and allowing no room for his recovery. You need to use the blood and name of Jesus Christ.

Playing the defense is needed at times, but do not let this be the place where you reside. You must take a stand in your choices. I choose to praise God amidst my struggles. This was not always so for me. However, the different battles I faced in my life took me to various emotional places. I encountered the mighty hands of

God lifting me from my turmoil, and that is why I stand today. No struggle is wonderful while going through it but coming out of it will give you something to look back at. Once you have crossed over that threshold, you can breathe again. The circumstances may be so gripping, that you feel like you are struggling to breathe. You can rest in the assurance that God is always there for you. He is there fighting for you no matter what the situation may be. So, hold your head up high and live.

## *Personal Encounters That Test My Faith*

It was twenty plus years ago when I had my first test on my battlefield. I was battling with stomach pain from my college years. This pain robbed me of my peace and rest and often had me scrunched up in bed or on the sofa. The pain was so bad, it was paralyzing, and the medication only relieved it for a while. While putting my trust in man-made remedies, I failed to trust in God.

The Bible says a little child shall lead them (Isaiah 11:6) and the Word of God does not lie. One particular afternoon, I got home from work and the stomach pain was so bad, it had me glued on the sofa in agony. I was out of medication, so I prayed for help from God, but my faith was weak. As I crunched over on the sofa, the shadow of someone entered the room. I glanced up to see my son standing over me.

26

"What is wrong, mom?" He asked.

I told him how much my stomach was hurting. He was nine years old, and his countenance changed. He laid his hand on me and began to pray. He had faith and he was about to use it. His weapon was sharpened and ready for execution. He was taught well, and he did learn. I had failed my test because my faith was weak. I had this weapon of faith and had failed to execute it the right way. I was placing my faith in the medicine made by man and forgot God, by whose stripes I am healed.

As my son raised his voice and began to pray, my faith shifted into gear. I was no longer holding a pity party. I was no longer holding on to the lies of the enemy; my faith was being revived. As my son raised his squeaky little voice at that time, his prayer rang out: "The God in whom I trust, and the God who my mother believes, touch my mom and heal her, in Jesus's name."

Oh, a quiver of goosebumps flowed over me. I knew his faith superseded mine at that time. He used the phrase: "the God in whom I trust, and the God who my mother believes" and those words moved me to the ultimate faith in God, and I was healed instantly. The pain left my stomach, never to return. I had passed my first test in the healing virtues of God, and I held on to it. The truth did set me free. My eyes were dim by the pain preventing me from seeing my Lord and Savior, who said by His stripe I am healed. The weapon used here was faith and intercessory prayer.

The other experience I had that really put my faith to the test was one that persisted for a few months. My injury happened while I was lying in my bed. I decided it was time to pray but was too lazy to get out of bed to kneel and pray. I knelt in my bed to pray but as I was changing position, I lost my balance and began to fall off the bed. In trying to break my fall, I injured my hip.

The injury took the form of excruciating pain that hindered a smooth transition from standing to sitting and vice versa. I struggled for quite a while. I went to the doctor and had x-rays and ultrasounds done, and they could not find anything broken, so they attributed it to muscle damage. The treatment regime was pain medication, muscle relaxant, and physical therapy. I complied with the regime but was still in pain. The pain was so bad that it was affecting me when I walked.

I prayed, but I was not putting my full trust in God. Honestly, I knew He could heal me, but I was not placing my all in Him at that time, and that was my problem. Jesus was not going to show up and heal me with half a belief. He wanted my full trust, holding nothing back. Can you relate to this?

My healing came when I put my complete faith in God. This happened after a Sunday service. I had gone to church that day and worshiped as I thought I should. I even went up for prayer when there was a call for those in the congregation who needed healing in their bodies. After being prayed for, there was no change. The pain was still rocking my hip after walking back to my seat. It was still there at the end of the service and I thought: "Lord, I really don't want to leave the same way I came today." The pain was becoming unbearable.

As I was about to leave the church, a brother approached me and said, "No woman of God should be walking this way." He asked if he could pray for me. I said yes because I was ready for my healing. The prayer was short but powerful. It felt like fire running down my hip to my toes. I was lifted off the ground by the Spirit, about two feet in the air. When I landed on my feet, I had no pain at all. I danced under the anointing of the Holy Spirit. What a jubilee that was for me. Jesus did it again; no more medications for me. As I am writing this testimony, I had never experienced that pain again. I realize also that, sometimes, for manifestation to occur, someone else's faith must either be equal to yours or above in believing together for a move of God.

Do not be like me and allow your lack of faith to prevent your breakthrough. Let go of the things you are holding on to and allow God to work in your life. It is your faith that moves the hand of God. When all have failed in the eyes of a man, God will step in. God will not share His glory with another; all glory belongs to Him.

Where is your hope? Who do you call on in your time of testing? Let your petition be known unto God. Launch out into the deep, so you can swim in your faith.

# Chapter 2
# The Obstacles Of Healing

If you are stuck with your first test, it is time to put your faith to the test. There may be challenges preventing you from moving into the realm that God wants for you. These challenges can be diverse and vary from person to person. Regardless of what your circumstances may look or feel like, God is here for you. The hurdles the enemy may place in your path can slow you down, but they will not stop you. Let us look at a few of these obstacles.

## *Fear*

Fear often plagues people to the point where there is no trust in God. The enemy brings to the mind different things to keep you in bondage to fear. You must not fear illness in any form, whether it is pain or a disease process that has come on you. You must trust God to take that away. The enemy wants you to believe that if your parents had it, you should too. The enemy may even say, "Everyone your age has it, so what is the big deal!" He wants you to accept that which is not meant for you. This ought not to be so. When fear is the main focus, you will forget to ask of God and may ask amiss. Matthew 7:7 states that we should ask, and it will be given.

The fear of "what ifs" will prevent you from taking hold of the promises of God. There are no "what ifs" with God. God will do that which He said He will do. His words are pure and purified. God cannot lie. In pushing forward in our minds, we put the Word of God into action. We speak to the possibilities. As children of God, we are not given the spirit of fear, but one of boldness. God gives us a spirit of peace, not as the world giveth. He brings hope and joy so we can join with the writer and say, "...The joy of the Lord is my strength" (Nehemiah 8:10).

There is the fear of letting go of what you already known and embracing what God has to offer without seeing it. The natural human tendency is to continue in the know because it feels good. Fear will have you rooted and not allow you to move into your destiny. Fear will not let you change your perspective on your circumstances.

## *Doubt*

The enemy brings doubt to the heart at the time of testing. Doubt is not of God. God wants us to trust Him. Proverbs 3:5-6 says we should trust in the Lord with all our heart and lean not to our own understanding. We need to acknowledge that God can do the extraordinary; that He is the keeper of our souls and cares about every aspect of our lives. He is the one who said we should cast all our cares on Him. God cares about our affairs. You may find yourself in diverse places in your walk with God, yet He changes not. His words are pure and have been tried in the furnace of the earth, purified seven times and without blemish. Therefore, it will accomplish that which it should. He also said He cannot lie because He is not like a man.

> *God is not a man, that he should lie: neither the son of man, that he should repent: hath he said, and shall he not do it? Or hath he spoken, and shall he not make it good?* (Numbers 23:19).

The enemy will come to you with lies, for example: "You are not going to get out of this" "Deliverance is not for you" "Oh, that is of the past. God does not do that anymore." These are all lies from the pit of hell. God is still in the healing and deliverance business. The Scripture says He changes not (Malachi 3:6). He is the same yesterday, today and forever. The Bible also encourages us not to be double-minded but focus on who God is and not to allow doubt to cloud our minds (James 1:8). If a man is unstable, he is like a volcano and he can erupt at any time. He is neither reliable nor trustworthy. You must make up your mind as to what you truly stand for.

The many testimonies cannot all be a lie. There are more testimonies of God's greatness in this world from the beginning of time. God sure does have His credibility, so you can put your trust in Him. We must be true to ourselves by acknowledging that nothing or no one can transform our lives, except Jesus Christ. He came to set the captives free (Isaiah 61:1 and Luke 4: 18). He came that you may have life more abundantly.

Your level of captivity may vary from another; it may be your health, family or finances. You may find yourself in situations, in different areas of your life, which seem impossible. It is time, therefore, to look to the One who delivers, Jesus Christ. Jesus is ready and waiting to set you free. The enemy will try to convince you that you are not worthy to be healed or delivered. You need to remind him that God did not mention anything about being worthy to receive anything. God loves us so much that He sent His only begotten Son to die for our sins.

There is an irony with the mental spell that the enemy tries to cast on the vulnerable. The enemy will bring people to a place of self-indulgence in self-pity, so they cannot see themselves as God sees them. God already paid the price for our sins on cavalry, so we should rejoice in Christ Jesus. Let us glorify Him who has paid the price.

> *But he was wounded for our transgression.* (Isaiah 53:5a).

As a child of God, it is your right to claim what your Father has given to you. He has given hope, peace, and faith in Him. It is His blood-coverage over us that made it possible for the impossibilities in our lives. Walk as children of God, with your heads held high, knowing that our Father is the King of kings.

## The "I" Factor

Where there is flesh, there will always be the "I" factor. The famous Psychoanalysis, Sigmund Freud, spoke about the "EGO" in the psychosexual stage of development. He described it in the latent period at age six to puberty. His theory states that this is where intellectual pursuits and social interaction develops. It is in this stage that social and communication skills and self-confidence emerge. It is a fact that his theories are controversial today. However, there must be some truth

35

to the word "ego." The dictionary defines ego as a person's sense of self-esteem or self-importance. The urban dictionary said it this way: "the ego is responsible for hate, fear, and delusion" (Urban Dictionary 2005).

We have an ego and we need it to function. However, there can be too much of it. Often, the phrase is used that one is "full of themselves" in reference to them having too big of an ego. Essentially, they are allowing themselves to dominate without much care. How does the ego relate to this book? Let us go back in time, to the Garden of Eden. According to the Bible, when Eve was tempted by the serpent, it was her self-awareness that allowed her to eat the forbidden fruit. The serpent beguiled her with words that played on her ego.

> *For God doth know that in the day ye eat thereof, then your eyes shall be opened, and ye shall be as gods, knowing good and evil.* (Genesis 3:5).

This was the first time the enemy defeated mankind with pride. The story goes on to say that when the woman saw that the tree was good and that it was pleasant to the eyes, and a tree to be desired to make one wise, she took of the fruit and did eat (Genesis 3:6). The desire to be equal in knowledge with God superseded the will to submit to God. The heart was enlarged with the feeling that "I" can now be wise. Eve wanted only to gratify the desires that plagued her. She wanted to be in control, to know it all. She wanted to be able to discern right from wrong. She wanted to become a god, as the serpent stated.

It is the sin of pride that separated man from God, and it is still at work now in the hearts of many. If you allow pride to take control, you will lose sight of God and there is little to no communication (prayerlessness). This wedge can only be broken when man yields to God. Pride aligns itself with arrogance and loftiness. The Bible speaks about this with Moab, who had magnified himself against the Lord. Moab thought he had it all, so he would not humble himself in the presence of the Lord.

> *We have heard the pride of Moab, (he is exceeding proud) his loftiness, and his arrogancy, and his pride, and the haughtiness of his heart.* (Jeremiah 48:29).

Loftiness speaks of being exalted in character, style or tone. It also makes excessive or unjustified claims. This is false pride, a sense of self-importance. While arrogance, as the dictionary defines it, is the state of acting superior or self-important in an offensive manner, it lines up with haughtiness and being egotistic.

God is intelligent and wants us to be. If we were made by Him and in His image, we should have all that and more. However, God also commands us to have no other god beside Him. Therefore, when we find ourselves in the state that Moab did, we have now found ourselves wanting to supersede the Lord, who is the Creator of all things. God made man from dust; think about that.

The humility is in submission to the Lord. This submissive state will allow us to accomplish the impossible, through the Lord. The Lord wants us to submit all to Him and worship Him in spirit and in truth. Hence, pride has no place with God. The book of Proverbs speaks about pride and its destruction:

> *Pride goeth before destruction and a haughty spirit before a fall. (*Proverbs 16:18).

> *A man's pride shall bring him low: but honor shall uphold the humble in spirit.* (Proverbs 29:23).

This verse strikes me the most:

> *The wicked, through the pride of his countenance, will not seek after God: God is not at all in his thoughts.* (Psalm 10:4).

Pride will hinder us from obtaining what God has in store for us. The prideful, arrogant heart will not ask God for what is needed, due to the heart being full of self and thinks self can accomplish it. There is no seeking or searching for God, so His favor will not be granted. Matthew 7:7 says, seek and ye shall find, ask and it shall be given. It is, therefore, imperative to ask of God. The "I" factor will hinder you from receiving your deliverance from God.

It is time for you to take a self-check. The question is, "Are you willing to give up your 'I' factor, so God can work miracles in your life?" There is no limit to what God can do. The Bible speaks about various miracles that God did, but miracles are not only done in the Bible. As you are reading this book, miracles are happening. He is working in someone's life right now and, maybe, working in yours too. The testimonies are endless.

# Chapter 3
## Put God First

*But seek ye first the kingdom of God, and his righteousness; and all these things shall be added unto you.* (Matthew 6:33).

The Lord our God created us in His likeness and for the purpose of worshiping Him. From the beginning of time, God loves to communicate with man, and this was evident in the book of Genesis when God visited the man in the evening for a talk (Genesis 3:8). It was a time of sweet communion between God and man, and that was ripped apart when sin entered the world. Sin made man self-conscious, and the man began to see himself more valuable than God. Adam and Eve started to focus on their own image and lost sight of the relationship they had with God.

If you put anything before God, you will lose what God has in store for you. God wants to give you what He has in store for you, but He will not, if you have closed the doors for your blessings. Adam and Eve were thrown out of the Garden of Eden because of their

41

disobedience to God, and their failure to acknowledge that they had done something wrong. They began to play the blame game. Have you ever found yourself in that situation? Be honest with yourself. We often blame others for the bad things that happen in our lives, instead of taking responsibility. It is time to take responsibility, so things can change. For every action, there is a counteraction. You cannot break the regular laws, and not expect punishment. Yet, with God, mercy prevails. The good news is, we have grace because of the blood of Jesus Christ. God does not want us to miss out on the blessings He has for us. He is the good Father, and He is even better than our earthly father, therefore, He will give us what we ask for.

We need to acknowledge when we are at fault and ask God's forgiveness so that grace may abide. Adam and Eve broke the Lord's commandment, and they expected no punishment. They did not show ownership, so they could not get forgiveness. Don't be caught in this situation. Matthew 7:7 says we should ask, and it will be given. We do not want to miss out on God's mercy because we pass on our errors to others. The Lord wants us to put all our burdens on Him. Psalm 55:22 says we are to cast our burden on the Lord, and he will sustain us. God wants to be there for you. He wants to ensure your every need is met. This cannot be accomplished, if you do not see Him as the most important person in your life.

We need to develop a daily relationship with Him. We must not take the simple things in life for granted, for example, waking up each morning. We can get caught up in what we must do for the day and miss the opportunity to say thank you to God. We forget to ask Him for guidance throughout our day. This is not what God wants; He wants to reason with you. Telling Him about the things that hurt you is important to Him. Discussing your plans with God before you do them will give you clarity and guidance. It is that kind of relationship, knitted so tightly that nothing can break it, that God seeks. He wants us to put Him first. He even said He is a jealous God (Deuteronomy 4:24). God made it simple for us: no other gods before Him. We must see God as paramount in our life, and that will push us closer to Him. Therefore, when you know who you are in Christ Jesus, you can lay hold on that which He has in store for you.

## My Youthful Experience

I recall my youthful days pressing towards a higher education after leaving high school. The struggles were real for my mother. She had other children to finance through high school, and it was not easy. I understood her financial constraints when she told me she could not afford to send me to college. Yet, I was adamant that I must achieve what others in my family did not, which was a college education. I decided to place all my trust in God. I had recently received the gift of the Holy Ghost in my final year of high school, so I was trusting in my heavenly Father. The beauty of it all was trusting God for the unknown. God specializes in things that seem impossible, and my situation seemed impossible. God said His ways are higher than our ways (Isaiah 55:9). Someone may have observed my circumstances then and thought how foolish I was, not knowing what I was going to do if I was accepted at a college. Where would the tuition fee come from? I had no family to help.

I was two weeks late in seeking out how I could attend college. I had no knowledge of how I would pay for college or what I was going to say as it relates to payment. The day before I had planned to go visit a college, my grandmother gave me money to pay for transportation to and from that college, and that was all I had. The next morning, I got up and prayed. I was trusting in the highest God and determined to break a cycle of the haves and have nots, the only way I knew how. God will be your reason when there is no other. He is our help in times of trouble.

When I arrived at that college, I met a lady who was dressed in white. She was very polite, and her greeting was complimented with a smile. She was eager to help me when I told her I wanted to attend college. She asked what subjects I did in high school and I told her the sciences. I was not expecting the conversation that proceeded. She asked me if I was interested in the nursing program. I answered in the affirmative, knowing it was my desire to pursue a career in healthcare. I asked her about the tuition fees as if I had money. I already knew my financial situation, but I was not willing to let down my guard of faith. She turned to me so gracefully and said, "It will cost you nothing. As a matter of fact, you get a stipend each month." I did not hesitate to say yes. It was an answer to my prayer. The door of opportunity was opened to me. To God be the glory! Who could it be but God?

When we allow God to go before us in everything we do, there will be a reward of good fruits. I went to that college with only hope and trust in God, no tuition fee, yet, I left enrolled in a program that led to a career in giving. I had accomplished in God what I could not for myself or by myself. God was working it out. I found favor in Him. I was not only going to college with my tuition paid in full, but I was getting money every month. God is awesome! He provides open doors and blesses.

> *Trust in the Lord with all thine heart, and lean not unto thine own understanding.* (Proverbs 3:5).

My youthful years in college became one blessing after another. As I reflect on my life, I realized that God was always with me and He was always delivering me from various situations that I encountered in my life. Let me share with you a few more awe moments for me.

## *The Enough Experience*

I was doing a post-graduate course and had to travel from school to home. I was a fulltime student and had all the responsibility of the school, as well as family. I was low on money. I was also low on gasoline. My white Nissan sunny was a manual shift car, with a two-liter engine and it was tailored to hug the road. I was approximately ninety minutes from home, with less than a quarter tank of gasoline. To be exact, the gauge was a few strokes above the E (empty). I had a conversation with myself, and I am not crazy. It was about my options to get more gasoline. Then I had a conversation with God.

I was passionate in my talk with the Lord and I was clear as to where my faith stood. I told God of my trust in Him to bring me home safely. I told Him I had no money to buy gas, and I was not going to beg or borrow. I told God I did not want to run out of gasoline on my way home. I knew the Lord could fuel the car, so I drove home as I would normally, while reminding God that He was in control. The Lord stunned me with His amazing miracle. He allowed me to drive home safely and the gas gauge did not move. What an amazing God! He works on our faith and He honors His Word. He said we shall not be borrowers (Deuteronomy 15:6). I trusted God for my deliverance, and He showed up.

As I reflected on that talk with God, I realized that it was more of a demand than asking. I was telling God what I wanted. I was bold in my talk with Him. I had confidence that He is a God who honors His Word. He said we are lenders and not borrowers, so why should I go find someone to borrow from? Why should I beg? Jesus promises to supply all my needs and I knew I could take that to the bank. I made a withdrawal from my faith deposit.

### The Supplier Experience

I remember traveling from Kingston Jamaica to Saint Ann Jamaica one evening. I had a new car, a Honda Accord. It was late in the evening and I was traveling alone. The enemy showed up his head, but it was all for God's glory. God will allow the enemy to set you up, but that set up is only for glorifying the Lord God, who is almighty and all-powerful. As I was going on my journey, I noticed the temperature gauge going up, so I stopped to check the radiator. The water was low, so I poured water into the radiator, and continued on my journey. The same thing started to happen again. I repeated the same routine. At that point, I just wanted to get home. I was concerned that it was dark, and I was traveling alone, so I just wanted to get home as soon as possible.

For the third time, the temperature gauge went up, but this time it went all the way to high. I was in a secluded area with no civilization in sight, and I was not going to stop in the dark, in the middle of nowhere, with bushes on both sides of the road and no lights. I did what I know best; I called on my Daddy. I prayed to God while driving. I said, "God, I am in the middle of nowhere and I am not going to stop on this road, and I refuse to be burned up in this car." As I finished that short prayer, I saw the temperature gauge going down, until it was at the normal range. I gave God praises for what He had done. I was not out of the red zone yet. As I neared a gas station, I was prompted to stop and check the car, so I pulled into the gas station. I switched off the engine, and a voice said, "Go buy a large coolant." I popped the hood of the car so the engine could cool down. I knew I could not pour coolant in a hot radiator.

As I walked towards the service area to purchase the coolant, I looked in my wallet and I only had the precise amount of money for the large coolant. I was reluctant, at first, because I would be left without money. I walked up to the salesperson and I was about to order a small coolant when the voice said, "Buy a large one." This time I obeyed, even though I pondered why I needed a large bottle. I learned that an empty radiator would accommodate a full gallon of coolant.

When the radiator cooled down, I poured the coolant in, and it took all of it. It was really dry. I still did not know what was really going on, but I knew that a car could not drive on a dry radiator without subsequent problems. I was about to close the hood, when the voice said, "Don't close it. Go and start the engine." I was in for a surprise. I started the car, and the coolant was spraying out. When I investigated, I found a severed radiator hose at the connection where the clamp was. I realized that I was really driving on a dry radiator all the way through the bushes for over forty minutes. God did it again. He showed up and did the impossible. There is no way I could have made it, if God was not favoring me. A car cannot drive on a dry radiator, without shutting down or erupting into flames. But God! He is such an amazing God. He heard my prayers and chose to answer. His mercy extended to this wretched woman. Thank you, Jesus! Thank you for Your mercies.

# Chapter 4
## Unwavering Faith

*"Today I say, if I die, I die alone and if I live to see tomorrow, it is because of Jesus. But as I think, I will not die alone, I will die with Jesus."*

~ *Debbie Watson-Allen*

W hen I received my first pair of glasses, I had mixed feeling as the Ophthalmologist said that at my age, it is common for people to have an eye defect.

*"As the eyes grow slowly dim, my spiritual eyes will remain on Thee, oh Lord."*

~ *Debbie Watson-Allen*

I wrote some little quotes for myself, not knowing what was ahead. I was at the age where healthcare specialists predict different changes in the aging body. I had a clean bill of health, so far. I was active and, mostly, eating healthy. I did not drink alcohol or smoke any form of tobacco, and I did not participate in a life of reveling. I tried to walk the straight and narrow path because I am a child of God.

I had plans for my life, and I don't remember consulting with God about them. I was planning to take my professional career to another level and see where that would take me. I had no plans for a setback. As a matter of fact, I put in the preliminary work by pushing to position myself for that next move, but I left God out of the equation. God was not pleased with me. I had an awakening to the fact that God is still in control, not me. I thought I was all set, but God was about to ruffle my rose petals.

I went to do a mammogram, thinking all was well as usual. I was called in for a second scan because they said they needed clarity. I remained nonchalant about the whole situation. I even told the person doing my scan that it was nothing, just some dense tissues. The scan results came in, and they were still undetermined. The next step was to do an ultrasound and, possibly, a biopsy. I agreed to the whole thing, still with a mindset that this was protocols needed.

When the ultrasound was done, the doctor told me there is a need for the biopsy, because they saw something suspicious. I went ahead with the biopsy. The results took a while to come back but, finally, the call came to ask when I could come in to discuss the findings. I remained calm as I went to speak with the doctor, refusing to let anything move me. There were thoughts of chemotherapy and surgery, but my trust was in God, and I knew He is able. I said, "Lord, You are in control."

My mind went into high gear as I left the hospital. Who do I tell? How do I tell them? My husband was working out of town and he operated heavy equipment, so I did not want to tell him over the phone. My two sons were also working, and I was thinking of protecting them from the news. I felt hungry, so I stopped at a fast-food restaurant to grab a bite. I ordered something I always liked but the taste was bland. Who do I talk to? Jesus knew where I was, but I was a bit shaken. I thought about my pastor's wife, so I decided to drive by her home.

It was November, and my pastor and his wife had just taken the position in August of that same year, so God had strategically placed people in my path for support, and I did not see it at the time. As I pulled up to their residence, I realized that her car was not parked outside. Where could she be at a time like this? I sat in my car, wondering what next. My pastor came out and asked, "How are you doing?" He had no clue what I was going through, but that question felt strangely odd that day. I went straight for the jugular, "Where is your wife? I came to see her."

He said, "Okay. She will be back shortly. Can I help you with anything?"

I knew he sensed that something was wrong. I could not hold it in any longer, so I blurted out, "I just found out I have breast cancer." The next few minutes were blurry. I saw the expression on his face and my emotions erupted into tears for the first time. It seemed like forever, but it was just minutes when his wife arrived. We went to their house for prayer. The intercessory prayer offered on my behalf that day was so intense, that I felt the pull of my spirit, like an out of body experience. I trusted God for my healing, knowing His words are true.

I examined myself to see where my faith was with God. I had faced a variety of challenges in my life, but this was new territory for me. My family had a history of diabetes and hypertension, but never cancer. As shaken as I was, my faith in God and what He can do was not suppressed. As a matter of fact, my faith increased. I was determined not to let it get me down.

I had to tell my husband and children, and that was not easy. When I told my husband, I could feel the rip in his spirit. My husband was shaken because he had lost his parents to cancer. I was more concerned about him, rather than myself. He was a very supportive husband and I knew he would be there for me. He did not make any reference to his parents, but I knew how he felt about their passing. I think my children, on the other hand, could handle it.

My subsequent visit to the oncologist revealed the magnitude of breast cancer. I was told I had stage three breast cancer, and it was invasive. I was diagnosed as HER2-positive (Human epidermal growth factor receptor 2). This HER2 was rapid growth and tends to spread. The oncologist had a plan laid out for treatment and I was not ready for it. The proposed plan was to start chemotherapy right away because of the size of the cancer cells. I said, "No, not until after Christmas." I knew the side effects of chemotherapy, and I did not want to spoil that time of the year for my family or myself.

The process involved several different appointments. I had chemotherapy counseling and my husband was by my side for this. The one thing that stood out was the change in diet. I realized that the mistake I was making was not using the herbs of the land, as God puts it. I was determined to change my choices in food. They also talked to me about the many drugs to combat the side effects of the chemotherapy drugs. I thought to myself, "I am no druggist, Lord, so why so many drugs? I don't want to use them; they are only going to make me sick." I made a note to myself: "Minimal medication; only as needed."

In preparation for chemotherapy, I agreed to have a port placed to prevent damage to my veins, if they were accessed. The day of surgery for that was very emotional. I honestly walked into the hospital an emotional wreck. I was really struggling with my new reality. My husband was sitting beside me, but I still felt like I had no support. I felt lonely and scared. He had no idea what I was really feeling. I managed to gain some control, until the nurse stepped into the room and said they were ready. As I was getting ready, I felt the walls of my emotions caving in and I could not hold it any longer. The tears flowed. My husband held me, and the tears flowed even more. Only God knows how I felt at that time.

The next month was filled with different decisions and challenges. I had to decide with whom to share this new development in my life. I did not want to share with people who lacked the confidence that God is a Healer. I was very skeptical because I did not want people breathing fear into my spirit. I wanted to tell those who were willing to trust God with me. I wanted those who would tarry with me, so I decided to share it with my family and some dear friends. I shared it with friends that I could trust to be there for me. They are a set of friends who have shared previous hard times and situations that required strong faith.

My friends did not leave me to chance. They knew the value of intercessory prayer, coupled with fasting, so they decided to do three days of fasting and prayer on my behalf. I wanted to be a part of it. Some may think I was crazy for doing this because I was on medication and weak in body, but I had a pull on my spirit that was stronger than ever. My determination to lay it all down at the feet of Jesus was without reckoning. I was banking on my faith.

Once you are chosen by God for a test, just like Job in the Bible, you must go through it. I believe, like Job, God said to Satan, "Have you considered my servant Debbie?" I know who I am in Jesus. I embrace the fact that I am a born-again child of God, bought with the precious blood of Jesus Christ. I answered the call of God and I hold on to the power of His salvation and I am pressing forward. I am not going to turn back by the grace of God. I have been through so much in my life and God has come to my rescue so many times. This was another time that I would continue to trust Him.

Jesus said in John 15:16: *"Ye have not chosen me, but I have chosen you, and ordained you, that ye should go and bring forth fruit, and that your fruit should remain: that whatsoever ye shall ask of the Father in my name, he may give it you."*

It is an awesome privilege to be chosen by God to bear fruit and for that fruit to remain. One of the fruit of the Spirit is longsuffering. No one wants to go through longsuffering, yet, it is one of the requirements by God. Longsuffering will test the other fruit of the Spirit within a person, like going to battle. It is that which you have learned over time, and have put into practice, that you will utilize in the face of your adversities.

It is easy for a child of God, who is pushed into a corner or has decisions to make, to go back to what they are comfortable with. I had to learn longsuffering through a disease that has claimed the lives of many. According to the Center for Disease Control and Prevention (2019), breast cancer is the second most common cause of death among black women. I was not going to become another statistic, by the grace of God.

Job did not curse God and die, as his wife suggested to him, but he put his trust in God to the end (Job 2:9). The Bible says he held on to his integrity (Job 2:10). What will come out of you when you are stricken? Will the world see Christ within you or not? The fruit of the Spirit is love, joy, peace, kindness, goodness, and faithfulness (Galatians 5:22). When you are pressed, will you produce these fruits?

When a soldier is captured in battle, he holds fast to the secrets of his country. He remains faithful. God wants us to remain faithful to Him, regardless of our circumstances. Paul said he rejoiced in whatsoever state he was in (Philippians 4:10-11). The goal is to push yourself to that place where nothing from the adversary moves you to be less than who God has called you to be.

Your circumstances may come with a lot of pressure, and the human side of you will want to give in to that which seems easy. The human side of us will want to complain, sulk and give in to that which is oppressing. But I recall the Word of God saying: "Be ye transformed by the renewing of your mind" (Romans 12:2). As we feed our minds on the Word of God, the Word will come to our rescue in times that seem hopeless. We can rest assured that the Word of God is true, and it will be a source of comfort. We can remind God of His promises to us during those times, and lay hold on the promises of God for deliverance.

Joseph found himself in a pit, with no way out but up. It is time to look up to the One who created all things. He is in control of all. He will allow that which He pleases, yet, your petition to Him can change His will through mercy. The secret is asking for deliverance. Ask what you will, and it shall be done (Luke 11:9).

Longsuffering is never easy, but it will prove who you are over time. I have heard and seen some people who held on to their faith in God, even in the face of death. These people encouraged others who visited them, regardless of how they were feeling at the time. I chose to be this way. I expressed my renown faith every chance I got. I was determined to hold on to the very end.

## *Why Worry (12/28/16)*

*As my eyes opened, my mind remembers that tomorrow will be the day of my first chemotherapy. I sought comfort in the Word of God, and I found Isaiah 41:10: "Fear thou not; for I am with thee: be not dismayed; for I am thy God: I will strengthen thee; yea, I will help thee; yea, I will uphold thee with the right hand of my righteousness." My prayers seem to hit the floor, but I know God is real. I was able to share my concerns with a friend and got spiritual support. "I am an overcomer, in Jesus's name!"*

On the day of my first chemotherapy, I lay in bed and meditated on the goodness of Jesus. A brother in Christ also sent me encouraging words and brought to my attention Psalm 91. My personal devotion took me to Psalm 121:1-3:

> *I will lift up mine eyes unto the hills, from whence cometh my help. My help cometh from the Lord, which made heaven and earth. He will*

*not suffer thy foot to be moved: he that keepeth thee will not slumber.*

God is able!

# Chapter 5
# Whose Report Will You Believe

There will come a time when you must take a stand as to whose report you will believe. You will be faced with circumstances that press you to make that decision: whether to trust God or man. When we become born again children of God, who we believe should not be an option. The obvious answer is God.

Some people still allow their trust to be limited by what they can see. Trust is defined by the dictionary as believing in the reliability, truth, ability, strength of someone or something.[1] On the other hand, the Bible says we should trust in the Lord with all our hearts and lean not to our own understanding. The word "trust" is mentioned over 147 times in the Bible. God wants us to fully trust Him. We put our trust in a myriad of things, for example, family, possessions, doctors,

---

[1] Oxford Dictionary

equipment, and machines, yet our trust in God is limited.

How many times have you flown in a plane and trust that it would take you to your destination? I am sure you did not check the plane yourself to ensure that all was functioning well. You do not know all the parts a plane is made up of and how they function, yet you trust in it. If you have never traveled on a plane, surely you have driven in a car, bus or ride the train. You put your trust in these things without question. You trust in what man has made, and you do this daily. So, why question God; the Creator of the universe? The Bible did say you are not to trust your own but put your trust in God (2 Corinthians 1:9).

I get overwhelmed just thinking about the God who created the universe; the God who said, "Let there be" and there was. It leaves me in awe. This same God created us in His likeness. Therefore, we are specially made by Him. He knows the number of hairs on our heads; that is a wonder. This all-knowledgeable God knows our thoughts. He is touched by the feelings of our infirmities. Knowing all this, how can we not trust Him?

If your trust is only in what you can see, then you cannot obtain the full miracles and deliverance from God. God is a Spirit and human beings have only seen

Him as the only begotten Son. God put on flesh and died for the sins of man. If God is a Spirit, then we must trust Him as such. He will move and not be seen; He will speak and not be seen. There is one connection, however, that will make the difference, and that is the feel of God. His Spirit will dwell in you. The Word of God says: if we worship Him, we must worship Him in spirit and truth (John 4:24). There are no two ways about it. There is only one way: God's way.

## The Passion Of My Belief

My faith was tested in the year of my chemotherapy treatment. It was a battle fought on many levels. My Oncologist did not care to hear my testimony that God healed me. On my first visit to her, she examined me and could not palpate the lump that was supposed to be in my breast. I told her God had healed me, and she looked at me as if I was stupid. I did not care what she thought because I knew what God had done.

I was examined again, and the lump could not be located. She went to her computer to review the information, so she could ascertain where it was supposed to be located. She tried again to find it, but there was nothing. The next step was to get a CT scan and MRI done.

The results came back confirming that there was a lump in my right breast consistent with the ultrasound. So they were saying the cancer mass was still there and the line of treatment was laid out: get a port, chemotherapy counseling, and start chemotherapy for four months, then reevaluate. I requested another CT scan, and she said they don't recommend it until chemotherapy was completed. Man's plan was to shrink the cancer cells with chemotherapy and then surgery. I was also told that there were two lumps. I did not push for the scan to be done, even though it was within my rights to insist. When God is about to do something, He will allow a man to clear the way, so He gets all the glory. The world knows that chemotherapy does not cure cancer. As a matter of fact, they are still searching for a cure.

My next oncologist visit was like the first. The cancer lump in my breast could not be palpated. My answer was the same: Jesus healed me. This time, I wanted her to know the name of my God. I wanted her to know that I was not going to denounce my God. She asked me if I felt any lumps. I told her no and I was not owning any cancer. Even if she did not believe in God, when He was through walking me through the process, she will know that there is a God who heals.

When God chooses you for a battle, He knows who you are. The Word of God says that before you were conceived in your mother's womb, He knew you (Isaiah 49:1). God knows you by name. There is nothing made on Earth that God does not know. So, when you are put to the test, stand ready in the name of Jesus Christ.

I did not go through my battle alone. I had friends and family praying for me and interceding on my behalf. My pastor's wife dedicated her time and faith to me. She was there at every doctor's visit, praying with and for me. I was fearful of the side-effects of the chemotherapy drugs, and I did not talk to her about it, but God knew. She prayed against the side effects, and I believed God to answer. The two side-effects that I dreaded were vomiting and diarrhea, so my faith was focused on preventing those two. I failed to acknowledge the other side-effects, so I had to refocus my faith when I was faced with them.

I was certainly not prepared for the side effect that would leave me sleepless due to the agonizing pain. The side effect came in the form of heartburn. If you have had heartburn, you may be thinking, "What is the big deal?" Heartburn is often relieved by over-the-counter medication such as tums. I was not anticipating what was to come. The attack was vicious on my stomach. It felt like an 18-wheeler truck was sitting on my chest, and then it erupted in flames and there was no way to put out the fire. This attack came in the middle of the night, jolting me out of my sleep. I was calling out to Jesus. My prayer was, "Lord, come to my rescue. I cannot handle this." The relief was not instant, but God did deliver that night. The pain slowly went away. I held on to the fact that God is my Healer. I never wanted to lose sight of what God can do. You can be shaken by your situation, but do not dwell on it. Instantly take control of your thoughts and redirect them to the positive.

The testing of my faith continued over the months that went by. I powered through, by the will of my mind. There were times my body had no strength, but my mind was powerful enough to will my legs to move. My body became so weak from the chemotherapy, that I would lay down and my body felt like noodles to get up. It was during those times that I would hug myself and remind myself that I could get through it because God was on my side. I had no clue why God allowed me to go through that battle, but there must be a reason. I felt pressed at times, so I chose to inundate myself with gospel music or the audio Word of God. This helped me stay focused on God, and not my present ill-feeling. I also made a power drink from fruits and vegetables. The recipe included strawberry, raspberry, blueberry, baby spinach, and kale. I added an apple for flavor and a spoon of energy shake for energy. I drank this once a day.

I remember when I was losing my hair due to chemotherapy. My first reaction was hilarious. The first loss was a clean sweep from the scalp. It looked like someone shaved the area smooth. I had to prepare for the inevitable: I was going to be bald. What would I look like? Then I said to myself, "Get it together. You can do this." The Bible says a woman's hair is her glory (1 Corinthians 11:15), and I was not going to lose my glory. It was a bit scary, but the angel of the Lord encamps around those who fear Him (Psalm 34:7).

I do not know why the Lord allowed me to go through that disease. I asked all the relevant questions at that time. Is it to build my faith? Is it to build my family's faith? Is it to show others who God is?[2] Whatever the reason, I purposed in myself that He is the divine Healer, and I would continue to trust Him. I stood my ground, like the three Hebrew boys who were thrown into the fiery furnace. Even if God did not deliver me, I would trust Him. He is still God. Like Daniel, even though the enemy had passed a decree to try and kill me, and I was in the lion's den, God is still God, and He has never failed.

At the end of six rounds of chemotherapy, a scan was scheduled. This was it; I would finally have some proof that I was healed. The results came in, as I anticipated:

---

[2] Journal entry 01/14/2017

they were negative. There was no trace of the cancer cells. My God did it, and there was evidence. My oncologist was not in agreement that it was a miracle, but I held on to my faith in God that He is a Healer and He chose to heal me.

The doctors wanted to continue with their traditional treatment regime, but I was not. My husband, on the other hand, was not so keen on me refusing the other treatments. I was torn between my faith and my husband. I had to seek counsel. The fact that my husband lost his parents to cancer made it hard for him. I did not know where he stood in his faith through it all, so I wasn't sure what to do. I decided to go with a lumpectomy, to gain further proof that I was healed. I did this, so there was more evidence for my husband.

In order to prepare for this surgery, I had to get a guidewire placed directly at the spot where the cancer was supposed to be. When I did the biopsy, a clip was placed in the area, so that was going to be the landmark for the lumpectomy. I went to the breast center and had the guidewire placed under ultrasound guidance. The results came back from pathology; all negative. There was no trace of cancer cells. I rejoiced in my God. He did it.

It was not over, because man was not satisfied with what God had done. As a matter of fact, they could not wrap their minds around the awesomeness of God. They failed to acknowledge that God did it. They were like Theophilus in the Bible; almost persuaded (Acts 1:1). There are always people who will not believe with you but do not become distracted by them. Do not allow them to overshadow your faith in God. Doubters will always be there, so choose to stand amidst it all. I had to take a firm stand when I was faced with the decision to do radiation. I was adamant that I was not going to do it. Why would I want to do radiation, when there were no cancer cells to kill? Why would I want to insult my God, who had healed me? It was already done. I did not need to do any fixing up.

My husband insisted that I go through with radiation, and that was a challenge for me. I asked him who he was really placing his trust in. I said, "Honey, I don't know whose report you are going to believe, but I choose to believe God. I know God has healed me, and that is evident in the results." There are times you must stand up for what you believe, no matter who is opposing your trust in God. I prayed for healing and trusted God to heal me, and He did. I was not going to put that on the back burner, no matter the cost.

A Radiology Oncology Doctor laughed in my face when I told him God healed me, and I was not going to do radiation. He was pleased to tell me that there may be some small cancer cells on my skin that I was not

71

seeing, and radiation would get rid of it. I asked him for the evidence of what he was saying, and he had none. It was pure speculation. Radiation destroys both your cells and bones, causing weakness. Why would I want to do that? There was absolutely no benefit. The doctor also said that radiation is to prevent cancer cells from coming back. I asked him what guarantee he could give that the cancer would not return. He said there was no guarantee, but it works. I said, "Well, you have no guarantee, but I have a guarantee in Jesus because He cannot lie. That which He said He will do, that He will do." The doctor looked at me as if I was one crazy woman. I am crazy! I have crazy faith in Jesus Christ, by whose stripes I am healed. I am willing to take my chances with Christ, rather than radiation. If God allowed cancer to return, so be it. He knows best.

# Chapter 6
# Press Forward In Victory

The victory that is obtained is enclosed in who you are in Christ Jesus. Knowing you are a child of God is what propels you to embrace the blessings and victories through Jesus Christ. 1 Peter 2:9 says we should show forth the praises of Him who hath called us out of darkness, and into His marvelous light. Our circumstances may have placed us in areas of darkness, but God has brought us out. When you have experienced your breakthrough or healing, it is time to move on rejoicing. The Bible says the joy of the Lord is our strength (Nehemiah 8:10). The Lord wants us to rejoice in Him, so we must never stop trusting in who Jesus is. The Word of God is there for us to learn from and use as one of our weapons of defense. It is the Word of God that will continue to guide us and keep us rejoicing. As you press forward, your joy remains as you hope in Christ Jesus.

*And they that know thy name will put their trust in thee: for thou, Lord, hast not forsaken them that seek thee.* (Psalm 9:10).

There should be no undermining of the enemy and his tactics. You should not be naive about the enemy's attacks. When you experience your breakthrough, the enemy will continue to try and cast doubt in your mind. However, remain steadfast in your faith that God is a Healer, Deliverer, and Savior. Surround yourself with positive stimulations and motivation. Your positive stimulations will come in the form of songs, the Word of God and encouragement. This must be a conscious decision on your part. You will be called upon to make hard decisions, for example, rejecting anything that will corrupt your mind or soul. The things you entertain by your senses become a part of your spirit, and the fruit of such may not be what you like, so choose wisely.

My battle with breast cancer changed who I considered to be friends and those who I choose to take advice or encouragement from. I realized that some people were just extra baggage in my life, and they had no purpose or maybe their time and purpose for my life had expired. Too often we hang on to strange relationships when there is no profit in them. These relationships become burdens that cause stagnation in our spiritual growth in Christ Jesus. It may sound harsh, but what is the benefit of having friends, who are not on the same level of faith as you? You can talk to them but choose carefully what you share because they can kill your faith.

The choice of the elect in your life will push you forward into another realm of the spirit. There is no going back to the ordinary, but the extraordinary will become your norm. The time has come for you to demonstrate your faith by helping others to realize their worth in the kingdom of God and rise to their chosen battle. It is you pouring out spiritual medicine for their healing. It is not you doing the healing, but you are helping someone to position themselves for God's healing power.

In pressing forward, be on the lookout for those who will doubt the move of God. When Moses was sent by God to Pharaoh to let the children of Israel go, Pharaoh doubted the move of God because his magicians could perform some of the miracles that Moses did according to the power of God. God still demonstrated dominion over every miracle and left them stunned. Do not allow the doubters to steal your victory in Jesus.

Victory is not self-contained; it needs support from others. You will get support from your immediate and extended family. The family includes your church family, who are there with you, always encouraging you to hold on to your faith. Your church family will pray and intercede on your behalf, for God to keep you anchored in His love and salvation. Your immediate family will be there in prayer and will provide an ear for you to express your feelings.

One of the biggest hindrances to living in the victory of Christ Jesus is self. The self will keep wondering if the sickness is going to return. Every time self hears of someone else being diagnosed with cancer, it will think the same is going to happen to you. Be reminded that God has not given us a spirit of fear, but that of boldness. This boldness must be manifested in you pressing forward. Do not second guess your God. Do not even entertain the thought. Sometimes you need to look in the mirror, and rebuke self, speak to self and let self know that God is the One in control. Let self know that, yes, we do not deserve what God was done, but it is already done from the cross and by His wounds, by His bruises, and by His stripes, we are healed.

Let us run like the man who was cleansed from leprosy in Mark 1:42-45. He did not keep quiet but published it and spread it all over. We need to tell of the goodness of God; tell of His deliverance in our lives, so others will come running to the only true and wise God. How can a miracle happen in your life and you keep quiet about it? Tell it and tell it some more. I love to share my testimony with others of God's healing power. The

Bible says we overcome by the blood of the Lamb and by the words of our testimonies (Revelation 12:11).

## *Peace In Your Victory*

The peace we have in Jesus Christ is an inner peace that flows outwards. The Lord gives us freedom from the turbulence of life. The peace of God gives us a new grip on life to go on living, knowing we have hope in Jesus. The knowledge we have gained about who God is, and the power in His name will propel us forward. We also gain an understanding of who we are and our limitations. You are stronger in the face of discord or stress.

The Bible did say we should seek peace and pursue it (Psalm 34:14). This peace is in sync with Jesus, due to the constant relationship that we maintain with Him. We need to be on our guard, and not allow the enemy to gain access to our lives. This can only be accomplished by keeping a strong connection to the Lord God almighty. We should keep the Lord's commandment and be careful that we do. The Bible says we should be careful of nothing (Philippians 4:6). In all things, we should have awareness, because the enemy is cunning, and we do not know when he will attack.

There was a covenant made by the Lord according to Isaiah 54:10:

> *For the mountains shall depart, and the hills be removed; but My kindness shall not depart from thee, neither shall the covenant of my peace be removed, saith the Lord that hath mercy on thee.*

This is awesome! I encourage you to hold on to this covenant. The Lord paid the price for our peace, so we have all rights according to His blood. Do not allow the enemy to tell you otherwise. Hold on to the Word of God. There is no lie in God, so His Word is pure and true.

## Strength In Your Victory

> *The Lord will give strength unto his people; the Lord will bless his people with peace. (*Psalm 29:11).

If we are to live in the strength of the Lord, we must listen when God is speaking. Too often we get caught up in the cares of life, that we forget there is a Lifesaver on our lifeboat. We find ourselves looking at the raging waves of our lives, yet the Master of those waves is resting on our ship. Your strength is not really your strength, but God's strength dwelling in you. When we listen to God, we will hear His directions. It is critical that we listen, so we are guided to extract the voice of God from among the various voices in our ear. Let the barriers that hinder the voice of God be broken down. The barriers come in the form of distractions and interruptions, for example, the things that seem simple in life. Your emotions, for example, the emotion of fear or doubt, can also block that communication.

In pressing forward in victory, your strength will be tested, but listen when God speaks. The mode God speaks through includes:

- **His Word.** This could take the form of preaching, teaching or reading the Bible.

- **His whispers.** God speaks to us Spirit to spirit. We may have dreams and visions.

- **His people.** We often encounter people who advise us, according to the direction of God's Spirit. People will also be there to correct you and offer guidance.

# Chapter 7
## Powerful Scriptures About Faith

The Lord gave His Word as evidence of His commitment to us. Therefore, we can draw upon His Word for any given situation. The power lies in our faith that God can do all things.

> *And we know that all things work together for good to them that love God, to them who are the called according to his purpose. (Romans 8:28).*

Nothing in your life, as a child of God, is by chance but your every move is orchestrated by the mighty hand of God. He knows every move we make. So, when the rough times come, find the will of God in it. It is for His Glory.

> *For with God nothing shall be impossible.* (Luke 1:37)

We often think things are impossible because we are looking to our own strength and abilities. This should not be as a child of God; we must believe that He can because He made all things and He allows whatever He wills.

> *Trust in the Lord with all thine heart; and lean not unto thine own understanding. In all thy ways acknowledge him, and he shall direct thy paths.* (Proverbs 3:5-6).

Trusting in the Lord should not be something we do occasionally, but we should trust Him consistently. We should not trust God for one thing yet doubt Him for something else. He said we are to trust Him with all our hearts, and that is what makes the difference. If you don't know God, you will not trust Him, so get to know God in order to build that trust. God also said we should not lean to our own understanding. The thing is, our understanding is limited in comparison to the all-knowledgeable God. How awesome it is to take counsel from the One who created the universe. The temptation is not to rationalize how things will go or what will happen, but rather trusting God through the process. We do not want to entertain negative thoughts as negative thoughts will push pause on the miracle God wants to work in our lives. God wants us to call on Him in times of trouble and believe that He cares about us. It is also important that our beliefs are coupled with our actions. Our actions should take the form of positive speaking and demonstrating an optimistic attitude in our daily living.

> *(For we walk by faith, not by sight:)* (2 Corinthians 5:7).

Our walk with God is not a natural one; it is a spiritual walk, where our battles are fought and won in the spiritual realm before the effects of the battle are revealed in the natural.

> *And all things, whatsoever ye shall ask in prayer, believing, ye shall receive.* (Matthew 21:22).

The Lord wants us to ask for what we need. It is not just the asking, but our faith that will move the hand of God.

> *I will say of the Lord, He is my refuge and my fortress: my God; in him will I trust.* (Psalm 91:2).

We have an assurance that God is there for us. The word "fortress" suggests somewhere secluded and secured, where people cannot easily get in. A fortress is heavily guarded, so invaders cannot get in easily. According to Psalm 91:11, He gives His angels charge over you. Therefore, you are fully protected. You have your own guardian angels. What an assurance we have in Christ Jesus.

> *That your faith should not stand in the wisdom of men, but in the power of God. (*1 Corinthians 2:5).

It is in God's wisdom that we stand. We know His power of deliverance, and that keeps us pushing forward. There is no weakness in Him, but pure power to heal, strengthen and keep.

> *I can do all things through Christ which strengtheneth me.* (Philippians 4:13).

Often, we think we can do things on our own and end up in a mess. We should rest in the strength of the Lord, who will direct our steps. Our assurance in God is pure confidence.

> *Fear thou not; for I am with thee: be not dismayed; for I am thy God: I will strengthen thee; yea, I will help thee; yea, I will uphold thee with the right hand of my righteousness.* (Isaiah 41:10).

We have hope in the Word of God. The fact that God cannot lie, makes it even more amazing that we can rest in His promises.

> *The righteous cry, and the Lord heareth, and delivereth them out of all their troubles. The Lord is nigh unto them that are of a broken heart; and saveth such as be of a contrite spirit.* (Psalm 34:17-18).

You may be broken, but God hears you. You may be perplexed, but God will comfort you. God's promises are true, so we can cry to Him. He will hear, and He will deliver.

> *I am crucified with Christ: nevertheless I live; yet not I, but Christ liveth in me: and the life which I now live in the flesh I live by the faith of the Son of God, who loved me, and gave himself for me.* (Galatians 2:20).

When Christ is in you, your turmoil is no match for the One who conquers death. God spoke, and there was (Genesis 1). He is the great I Am, and nothing is impossible with Him.

> *Therefore I say unto you, what things soever ye desire, when ye pray, believe that ye receive them, and ye shall have them.* (Mark 11:24).

This Scripture was the one I focused on often, during the time of my testing. This helped me to keep my faith in God, knowing I had the opportunity to call on Him anytime. I felt comforted, knowing God cares about my desires when I pray, and I trust God to honor His Word.

# Allow God

Your life is in the hands of the Author and Finisher of your faith.

Your life was made with a direction. You have no idea where it is going, but that direction is paved for you and it is one you must walk.

It requires that you condition your mind to walk according to God's call on your life.

There is no road that is smooth. If it is too smooth, it is already setting you up for danger. So, your road will have some rough patches.

Your road will have some bumps to slow you down at times.

Your road will have some curves because the curves will take you in directions out of danger.

Your road will be narrow because the road you are walking is only fit for you and your Savior.

Your road is one that is directed by your Savior. He is the One who is in the front seat of your life.

Allow Him to drive you in your purpose. Allow Him to drive you where He has chosen for you to go.

Do not resist the arms of God on you. Do not resist the purpose He has for you. Let go and let God direct you to your elevation, purpose, and destiny.

You do not see it, but it is coming. Your faith will bring you through. Your faith will allow you to trust in God; to bring you to that place you do not see.

Your resting place is not yet; you are still on your journey. Your journey may be short, or it may be long; you do not know, but God is with you on this journey.

Allow God to direct your path.

Let God.

~ Debbie Watson-Allen

# About the Author

Debbie Racquel Watson-Allen is a born-again child of God and avid worshipper, purposed to do whatever she can for the glory of God. She accepted the Lord in her teenage life and faced many battles of faith. She is supported by her husband, Micheal, and sons, Dwayne and Taran Allen. As a steward of the Lord, she served in many ministries within the church, including Youth President and Assistant Missions Director. Her passion for the gospel of Christ took her different places sharing the love of God.

Debbie is a nurse by profession who has dedicated her life to serve. Her place of work is her mission field. She embraces this revelation and interceded for many in need of Christ. Her faith was put to the test when faced with breast cancer. She chose the winning side.

Made in the USA
Middletown, DE
23 June 2023

33014451R00056